Understanding & Supporting Autistic Students In Specialised Schools

I0117225

Paul Isaacs

chipmunkapublishing
the mental health publisher

Published by
Chipmunkapublishing
United Kingdom

http://www.chipmunkapublishing.com

Copyright © Paul Isaacs 2013

ISBN 978-1-78382-025-2

Edited by Lesley Kirk

About Chipmunkapublishing

Mental health books give a voice to writers with mental illness around the world. At Chipmunkapublishing we raise awareness of mental health and the stigma surrounding mental health problems by encouraging society to listen. We are documenting mental health literature as a genre so history does not forget the survivors and carers of people with mental illness and disabilities.

Chipmunkapublishing gratefully acknowledge the support of Arts Council England.

Chapters

Author's Introduction

Author's Introduction

© Isaacs 2011

I believe that Autistic people have the right to a productive and meaningful education that brings them happiness and joy, where their disabilities are understood and catered for and their abilities are encouraged and explored.

I have worked in an Autism base and also a school for students with Autism and Learning Disabilities through my own personal experience of education and also my observations of the educational environment for Autistic people.

The overall importance is happiness and for the students to have the right to be themselves.

The Myth of Mild Autism

This subjective term comes from a misunderstanding of Autism Spectrum Disorders in general. This can be very damaging to people on the spectrum whose difficulties are considered "mild" as a variant which is conclusively wrong.
If someone has a diagnosis of an ASD (Autism Spectrum Disorder) that means they have pervasive difficulties with social communication, sensory issues, learning difficulties and language problems, regardless of any other additional issues present. People with Autism are confused by the world around them despite what diagnosis they have.

Different ASD diagnoses will be used such as

- Autism
- Atypical Autism
- Pervasive Developmental Disorder (PDD)
- Pervasive Developmental Disorder Not Otherwise Specified (PDD-NOS)
- Asperger's Syndrome (AS)
- High Functioning Autism (HFA)

People may also have an additional diagnosis of a Learning Disability (LD)

Additional diagnosis may also be recognised

- ADHD (Attention Deficit Hyperactivity Disorder)
- ADD (Attention Deficit Disorder)
- Tourette's Syndrome
- Semantic Pragmatic Disorder
- Mutism
- Gut & Metabolic Disorders

Auditory Processing Disorder

Auditory processing in autism is complex. Many autistic people have a hyper (over) sensitivity to sound which causes great discomfort and physical pain. Further complications to sound can cause headaches, migraines, anxiety, communication difficulties, meltdowns, shutdowns and challenging behaviours.

Sound Avoidance

- Will avoid and be scared of certain sounds (phonophobia)
- Will run away and avoid certain places and areas
- Will put their hands or their fingers in their ears to drown the sound
- Will make further noise to drown the oncoming bombardment of sounds
- Will become highly anxious, stressed and upset in situations with certain sounds

However... The paradox is that they may have sounds they like to listen to and experience again and again. This creates enjoyment, comfort and a way of expression and calm for them. If you have sound sensitive hearing you have the ability to listen to sounds on a repetitive level.

Sound Seeking

- Will listen and play certain sounds (toys, videos, audio CDs, youtube etc)
- Self-educating themselves about sounds and words
- Will sometimes like to repeat sounds, phrases and words (echolalia)
- They may stim (move, flap, bounce) and be very active and animated whilst listening to their favourite sounds and clips

Remember

To always be person centred with the way in which you understand all the students and how they interact with people in the world around them. Always use a person centred profile to make them feel safe, secure and comfortable and the ability to be true to themselves.

Autism & Emotional Processing

85% of people on the autism spectrum have problems with self-emotional recognition (Alexithymia). This can cause problems with thinking and being aware that situations are alright when they aren't. This can also have an impact on how autistic people generalise a situation, cope with changes and how they react to other people's behaviour.

Alexithymia is defined by

- Difficulty identifying feelings and distinguishing between feelings and bodily sensations of emotional arousal
- Difficulty describing feelings to other people
- Constricted imaginable processes, as evidence by a scarcity of fantasies (although I do believe people with Autism have really deep imaginations)
- A stimulus-bound, externally oriented cognitive style

This is a problem when students with Autism try to describe their feelings towards a situation because from a processing point of view they're not "there" and will not be able to recognise an emotional issue (happiness, sadness, agreement, disagreement) within a situation they have been in. Be aware to give the student lots of processing time and when they are ready to communicate their issues give them time to extract information.

Autism & Depression

Depression is something that anybody can get in their lives due to a multitude of reasons such as emotional grief or a serious illness for example. With many processing and environment issues that come with having Autism, the question is would it be "easy" to spot if a person with Autism is unhappy and have clinical depression? Some of the reasons will be Autism specific. Here are some examples of what could contribute to mental illness.

- Not being understood by family, peers or staff members
- History of bullying and teasing
- Communication profile not being taking into account
- Sensory issues not being recognised nor taken into account
- Communicating being a struggle on a daily basis
- Auto-Immune and Metabolic disorders causing discomfort and pain
- Brain working "overtime" due to emotional and processing issues
- An autistic person being denied their special interests
- Lack of support and understanding by others

These issues will of course overlap with the non-autistic population which is good in many respects because these are all human emotions and basic human rights, needs and wants which everyone deserves. However as you can see from some of the bullet points they are very much Autism specific in how the person views, perceives and reacts to the world and these should be acknowledged by the staff around the person, and this can have a vital and dramatic effect on the Autistic person's mental health. Remember to always understand what is going on from the "inside" in order for the Autistic person to be happy, safe, secure and ultimately understood.

Autism & Language

Autism and language can be split into two parts

Expressive

Expressive language can be shown in many different ways. It may be through route language and echolalia (with acquired meaning) for people who are verbal on the Autistic spectrum. This doesn't mean that it is easy for someone who is verbal to speak because the difficulties with communication are still very much present and assumptions about difficulties should not be present if someone can speak nor should a person who is non-verbal be "written off" just because they cannot verbalise. Other methods of communicating can be shown through sounds, movements and gestures for people who are non-verbal. This is very important and can be frustrating for them to show their emotions, opinions and views. This can be helped through facilitated communication (FC) which can help the internal world of a non-verbal Autistic become external. Also note that expressive body language may not reflect always what the Autistic student is thinking or feeling. Recognise patterns of behaviours that represent true thoughts and feelings.

Receptive

Receptive language can be difficult and can affect how someone reacts to a situation. This is an issue that affects people on the whole of the Autistic spectrum. Please understand that a receptive language difficulty doesn't reflect intelligence but receptive understanding. If a person is meaning deaf and only processes a few words of a sentence at a time, make your sentences clipped, concise and clear. If someone is very literal and has a semantic pragmatic (literal use of) language, please do not use sarcasm, irony, or tone because these things will not be picked up nor processed. Building bridges of communication is very important for both staff and the Autistic students.

Autism & Scotopic Sensitivity Syndrome

This is a syndrome which was recognised in the 1980s by Helen Irlen for people diagnosed with dyslexia and visual related learning difficulties. In 1995 Donna Williams documented how tinted lenses helped her perceive the world better. This documentary was called "Jam Jar" and she also documents her lenses in her third autobiography "Like Colour to the Blind".

Here are some of the symptoms of visual fragmentation which can affect people with Autism and other related learning and developmental disabilities.

- Face Blindness (not recognising faces because they are fragmented)
- Object Blindness (not processing objects or people)
- Meaning Blindness (not processing the meaning of things)
- Context Blindness (not processing or interpreting context)
- Comprehension Blindness (problems with processing words)
- Poor Depth Perception (not understanding foreground and background)
- May not have a visual memory
- Distracted or disturbed by lights, colours or shapes
- Suffer from headaches or migraines
- May have poor Math skills (dyscalculia)
- May have poor Writing (dyslexia)
- May perceive the world in a "Sensory Based System"

Autism & Employment

Employment can be very difficult for people on the spectrum. This can be to do with many factors of work such as sensory issues, communication issues and understanding what the staff want out of the person with Autism in terms of work productivity for example.

Remember that work and achievement are important for people on the spectrum and the students will need a lot of specific support from staff and also the people within the workplace. Here are some ways to help the students achieve this.

- What would they like to do? Give them options remember "bottom up" thinking (T.Grandin) and giving the students clear concepts
- Assisting them with understanding application forms and information sharing. The students may need assistance with filling out these forms from a staff member. This will take time to do because of processing receptive and expressive language

Job Interviews

I believe that everyone on the Autistic spectrum deserves the chance to have a job. Interviews should also be person centred with help from the staff. Sensory considerations and information processing should be taken into account.

Within the Job

The Autistic student within the job will need concepts explained further such as.

1. Job Role
2. The Jobs within the role
3. Work mates and boundaries
4. Work productivity
5. When difficulties arise who do they go to
6. How am I doing? (People with Autism have no concept of how they're doing and need to be told)

- Other issues around extra work breaks, work hours and sensory issues could also be worked upon to make the job more accessible for the person with Autism. As well as a need for support and crisis management.

- Giving the students a choice is important as this will build up their social skills, confidence and empowerment in a person centred friendly manner. It will also give them a chance to experience employment with the right level of support, guidance and help.

Autism & the System of "Sensing" Vs Interpretation"

For some people with Autism the system of sensing before interpretation can be a system they live with all their lives. This can be both very challenging and liberating for a person with Autism to live in (as I do on a personal level) but it can create confusion with not only the person themselves but also the people they meet and interact with. Please be aware this is a way of being for many people and may well reflect what you're seeing on the outside.

Here is an example I often use in my speeches to make people think about interpretation and sensing.

"Imagine a baby looking at a set of lights from a toy you have given it and the baby seems to be enjoying the sensory input."

"Does the baby know what the plastic is made of?

"Does the baby know what company the toy is made by?"

"Does the baby know what lights are powered by?"

"The answer to these questions is probably **no.**"

As Autism is a developmental disability some people are living, experiencing and perceiving in this sensory based system/world. This doesn't mean they lack intelligence but it does mean they react to the world and explore it in a very different way as a result of this system.

Picking Up on the "Vibes" of the Environment

People with Autism and Learning Disabilities can pick up on "positive" and "negative" vibes in a situation. It is important to create a positive, happy and person centred environment for both students and staff.

The students will pick up on negative energy and very quickly this can cause problems with concentration, being in certain rooms with certain students and staff members. This can also have an impact on the student's mood and mental health. Always remember that positive projection, surroundings and people are the key foundations for good practice in a school/ learning environment.

Here are some points of reference.

- Remember energy is important
- Be careful what you project and what you talk about in front of students (such as other students and staff members)
- Be aware the students may want to communicate how the energy is making them feel
- Positive energy will give the students confidence and then their true abilities will show

Autism & Body Disconnectivity

Some people with Autism may have a disconnection with the physical environment but also the environment of their own bodies and how they're connected from the head, neck, arms, legs and hands etc. This can cause a sense of "floating" for some people with Autism and this is very much an "internal" sensory perception issue.

Here are some signs of body Disconnectivity.

- Knocking into things and not understating the physical space between things, people and themselves
- May like to wrap themselves in things such as blankets, jumpers, hats and weighted materials to get a sense of "self" and connectivity
- May hit themselves or parts of their bodies repeatedly
- May be they are a sensory seeker who needs to connect and feel things in order to connect and feel a part of themselves
- May smear faeces
- May liked to be hugged or like to be hugged by others
- May be "blind" to certain parts of their bodies and may need help with connecting. This may take time and also other issues such as mood, anxiety and processing need to be taken into account.

Autism & Stimming

It has many purposes such as

- Understanding the Environment
- Processing Emotions
- Processing Visuals
- Processing Auditory Senses
- Processing Body Connectivity
- A Form of Communicating

Christmas time for Autistic Students

Christmas time can be a very confusing and anxious time for students. Make sure that you understand the following aspects and the person centred profile of the students must be taken into account.

Be clear, no surprises about Christmas and what it entails. Cover all aspects of it such as.

- Presents
- Lights
- Decorations
- The Meaning of Christmas
- Remember that many Autistic students are "bottom up thinkers" they need a concept and Christmas is the concept
- This will help the students relax and feel safe, secure and happy

Visual Sensory Avoiders

- Strong dislike of visuals such as lights, tinsel and strong colours
- This can cause pain and discomfort
- Emotional anxiety and communicational "cluttering"
- Remember to give the students the freedom to remove themselves from a place which is causing sensory overload
- The communicational understanding of their needs will make them happier and secure
- Do not punish a sensory issue because it causes anxiety and further confusion for the student which isn't needed nor deserved

Visual Sensory Seekers

- Strong likes for intense visual stimulation, such as toys, lights, colours, shapes and fabrics etc
- These objects will make them relaxed and comfortable
- Creates emotional balance and stability
- Aids communicational skills when sensory input is put in place rather than hinders

- If they have an object that they like to use to spin, tap, twirl for example do not take the object away from them as it has a strong connected need which should be seen as a friendship
- Do not punish sensory seeking because it has a strong functional need

A Different type of Body Language Autism

Sometimes body language in a person with Autism can present itself differently than those who are not on the Autistic spectrum. This can cause problems with miscommunication with staff members and students, because sometimes the face and body of the Autistic student is not showing what is going on from the "inside". Here are some points to be aware of.

- Being aware that some facial expressions are learned by route
- Some people on the spectrum may cover up what they're feeling
- Some people on the spectrum may find it difficult to match the "emotion" with the "facial expression" and "body language"
- Some expressions and moods may be shown later because of emotional processing
- Body language may be different because of coordination issues
- Body language may be different because of sensory profiles
- Body language may be different because of dissociation issues (detaching from a place, situation and/or the self)
- The system of sensing may be higher than the system of "receptive" and "expressive" body language

Giving the Autistic Students a Concept

The ability to generalise concepts is hardwired into people without Autism. This means that a concept doesn't have to be explained in great detail because the generalised concept is available to be ported over from different situations. It is intuitive so generalising concepts is easier and quicker to process.

For people with Autism "bottom up thinking" (T.Grandin) is a processing issue so all specific aspects of a specific situation is needed to be explained in full, because the ability to port over and refine information from different situations is difficult to access, understand, process and initiate. Therefore a problem with generalising information.

Here are some tips and advice.

- What is the situation? Use a person centred communication profile to explain

- What changes will be made to the environment (list and describe all the changes before they happen)

- Give the students a choice of different aspects of changes to remember about their sensory profile and what impact changes will have on them. By giving students a choice this will give them the positive empowerment of choices and help them with self confidence

- Presents – Some people with Autism dislike presents because of the uncertainty of what is in the package which can cause huge anxiety for some students. A good idea would be to show the student the present and then wrap it up. This can be with shiny paper (for sensory seekers) or a plain packing (for sensory avoiders) again build up a concept of what a present is and what it means.

- By building an overall concept for the students this will make them feel safe, secure and reduce anxiety at times of change. Remember, it is not stubbornness that is the issue, it is the inability to see concepts and generalise

Reflective Thinking

Lock, Doors & Key Codes

Many challenges for the Autistic students are to do with the learning environment which they're in. One aspect of this is the function of many specialist schools locks, doors and key codes that are around many buildings as well as gates and barriers around many campuses.

Here are some questions that I would like people to reflect upon with regards to locks on doors in specialist schools.

- What message does this send out to the students?
- How could a student feel being aware that locks are on all the doors?
- How does this affect the student's learning?
- How does this affect the student's mood?
- How does this affect a student's transition?
- How does this affect the students overall association with locks and doors?
- What sort of message is this sending the student?

Concerns if a student escapes? Here are some to things to think over

- Why do they want to escape?
- Is it sensory?
- Home sickness?
- Students?
- Staff members?
- Feeling trapped?
- Boredom?
- Freedom?
- Stress and Anxiety?
- Mental Illness for example depression
- Or a mix of the things stated above

As staff, how would you feel if locks were put on the doors? What if other people had control of the doors and how they were used?

It's always positive and reflective to put yourselves as staff members into the shoes of the students and see it from their perspective, and hopefully it will make you think of how you would feel if the situation was reversed.

Differences between having a Learning Disability & an Autism Spectrum Disorder

Autism Spectrum Disorder

Problems with –

- Sensory Issues (both over and under sensitive)
- Communication issues (Literal Thinking/Meaning Deaf)
- Tone of Voice
- Processing facial expressions and body language
- Processing thoughts and feelings
- Generalisations and typical abstract thought (social imagination)

Learning Disability

Problems with-

- Communication for non-autistic reasons people with LDs can pick up facial expressions, tone of voice and can have better versatility at generalised thought. It's to do with content and direction.

- Expressing Emotions & Using Social Tools they may have a lot of social awareness but may get frustrated because they can't express their emotions in a typical way, give them the confidence to do so.

- Different Pathways of Learning. Like people who have Autism people with LDs are very intelligent people, their learning pathway is different because of their LD. If you tap into what makes them happy, feel enabled and less anxious it will create positive vibes for their self-worth and achievement.

Some people can have Autism and can be severely affected just as much as a person with a Learning Disability. Some people will get a dual (double) diagnosis of both Autism & a Learning Disability, who need the consideration of both communication and learning profiles.

Dissociation & Sensory Issues

As a potential coping mechanism for sensory (and of course emotional) issues a person with Autism can dissociate from the "world" around them, going into themselves or more accurately "away" from themselves and the situation they're in. If sensory bombardment has been going on for years and years such as shopping centres for example, it can become a tool to "get away" from a situation completely. Here are some points that relate to people on the Autism spectrum and dissociative disorders.

- Sensory processing
- Emotional & Physical trauma
- Lack of understanding of others
- Lack of understanding from other people
- Low confidence
- Low self esteem
- Mental health problems such as depression, bipolar disorder, anxiety disorder etc
- A Fantasy World seemingly more attractive
- A Fantasy Characters/Alters that become more prominent
- When their voice tone and/or body language and characteristics become different (this is ruling out developmental reasons such as echolalia and echopraxia)
- Interests switch dramatically and personality changes

Gut, Immune & Metabolic Disorders

There has been evidence that these disorders can overlap with people with Autism, this can be to do with related genetic disorder through the family genes such as

- Eczema/Atopic dermatitis
- Crohn's disease
- Coeliac disease
- Irritable Bowel syndrome
- Gluten, Wheat and other food intolerances

These are to name but a few but this can cause discomfort to people on the autism spectrum causing problems with speech, eating, lethargy (tiredness), concentration, mood and mental health.

Other symptoms may include itching of the skin, bad stomachs (vomiting, diarrhoea and/or constipation), stomach cramps, dizziness, headaches, migraines, self-harming, excessive itching of the anus (because of excessive mucus, fungal infection) this can cause anal fissure and further complications.

Specialist's can help with assisted diets which can help with many of the symptoms stated above.

www.ingramcontent.com/pod-product-compliance
Lightning Source LLC
Chambersburg PA
CBHW031221290326
41931CB00035B/664